BAKALEINIKOFF
Serenade

This is an attractive little piece with a rhythmic accompaniment which supports the trumpet very well. Be careful that the notes in the third and fourth measures move ahead and don't become static. One phrase must flow into the next.

This music offers a fine opportunity to play with a mute. Bakaleinikoff suggests a *mute dolce.* I used a normal straight plastic mute for the recording. Plastic, cardboard, or wooden mutes soften loud playing. If I had used a metal mute, the loud passages would have had a very nasal quality. Be aware that mutes usually sharpen the pitch; you will have to adjust accordingly. Bakaleinikoff has given the player plenty of time to position and adjust his mute.

This solo needs long, smooth notes. Play the triple tongued triplets as broadly as possible without altering the flow of the music.

DONAUDY
Aria No. 1 — Luoghi sereni e cari

The composer, Stefano Donaudy, wrote many songs in the style of the 17th and 18th Centuries. Be sure to observe the *tenuto* mark in measure 9; it is most effective.

DONAUDY
Aria No. 2 — Quando ti rivedro

Fitzgerald did an excellent job when he transcribed Donaudy's songs for trumpet. They lie very well, but do need breath control and smooth playing. Listen carefully to the accompaniment and play with smooth legato.

FITZGERALD
Italian Suite — First Movement: Allegro
(Alessandro Scarlatti)

This is a vigorous Tarantella with robust sound. The editor, Bernard Fitzgerald, has indicated many slurs. If all these eighth notes were tongued, the piece would sound very different. The section beginning at measure 27 is much more lyrical. You will need to practice the fingering in this part; it is rather difficult. If you need a breath before measure 39, you will have to shorten the previous note. The ending before the repeat could be done without a ritard. Observe the accents and play with strong support.

FITZGERALD
Italian Suite — Third Movement: Andante (S. De Luca)

This transcription is very vocal in style. Notice the conversation between the trumpet and the piano. It will be helpful if you know the accompaniment as well as the solo line. Observe all the markings; they are essential to an interesting performance.

FITZGERALD
Italian Suite — Fourth Movement: Danza
(Francesco Durante)

This is a brilliant song; it lies very well for the trumpet. Watch the phrase markings and work for smooth articulation. I added trills to measures 40 and 66 — you may wish to try them too!

COMPACT DISC PAGE AND BAND INFORMATION

MMO CD 3812
MMO Cass. 8032

LAUREATE SERIES CONTEST SOLOS
BEGINNING LEVEL FOR TRUMPET, VOL. 2

MMO CD
3812
MMO Cass.
8032

TUNING
Before the piano accompaniment begins you will hear four tuning notes, followed by a short scale and another tuning note. This will enable you to tune your instrument to the record.

MMO CD 3812
MMO Cass. 8032

TRUMPET VOLUNTARY

Compact Disc
Band 1 - With Trumpet
Band 12 - Without Trumpet

JEREMIAH CLARKE
Arr. by Clifford Lillya
and Merle J. Isaac

Cassette

Side B - Band 1 ♩ = 108 (3'23")

MMO CD 3812
MMO Cass. 8032

ARIOSO

Compact Disc
Band 2 - With Trumpet
Band 13 - Without Trumpet

J. S. BACH
Arr. by Walter Eckard

Cassette

Side B - Band 2 ♩ = 72 (2'33")

4 beats precede music

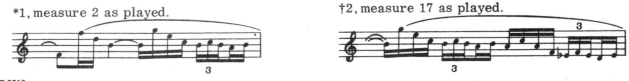

*Bach also made use of the same material in more ornamental style in the slow movement of his "Clavier Concerto" in F minor.

*1, measure 2 as played.

†2, measure 17 as played.

MMO CD 3812
MMO Cass. 8032

ARIA

Compact Disc
Band 3 - With Trumpet
Band 14 - Without Trumpet

ANTONIO F. TENAGLIA
Trans. by R. Bernard Fitzgerald

Cassette

Side B - Band 3 ♩ = 80 (1'50")

MMO CD 3812
MMO Cass. 8032

ALLEGRO

Compact Disc
Band 4 - With Trumpet
Band 15 - Without Trumpet
Band 16 - Without Trumpet (Slow Version)

JOHANN P. KRIEGER
Trans. by R. Bernard Fitzgerald

Cassette

Side B - Band 4 ♩ = 112 (1'19")
Side B - Band 5 ♩ = 72 (1'50")

MMO CD 3812
MMO Cass. 8032

10

SERENADE

Compact Disc
Band 5 - With Trumpet
Band 17 - Without Trumpet

Cassette

Side B - Band 6 ♩ = 116 (2'22")

VLADIMIR BAKALEINIKOFF

MMO CD 3812
MMO Cass. 8032

ARIAS

Compact Disc
Band 6 - With Trumpet
Band 18 - Without Trumpet

STEFANO DONAUDY
Trans. by R. Bernard Fitzgerald

Cassette

Side B - Band 7 ♩ = 63 (2'36")

3 beats precede music

Andante con Larghezza

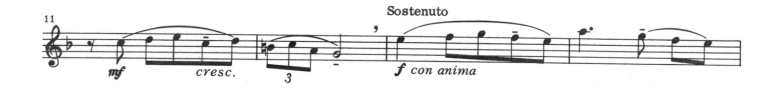

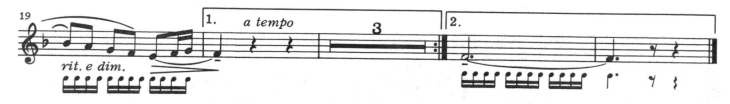

MMO CD 3812
MMO Cass. 8032

Cassette

Compact Disc
Band 7 - With Trumpet
Band 19 - Without Trumpet

Side B – Band 8 ♩ = 56 (2'13")

4 beats precede music

Largo

Poco più mosso

MMO CD 3812
MMO Cass. 8032

14

ITALIAN SUITE

Compact Disc
Band 8 - With Trumpet
Band 20 - Without Trumpet
Band 21 - Without Trumpet (Slow Version)

Cassette

Side B - Band 9 ♩.=126 (1'21")
Side B - Band 10 ♩.= 84 (1'42")

I Allegro

ALESSANDRO SCARLATTI
Edited by Bernard Fitzgerald

MMO CD 3812
MMO Cass. 8032

III Andante

Compact Disc
Band 9 - With Trumpet
Band 22 - Without Trumpet

S. DE LUCA
Edited by Bernard Fitzgerald

Cassette

Side B - Band 11 ♩ = 104 (2'24")

IV Danza

Cassette

Side B – Band 12 ♩. = 80 (1'03")

Compact Disc
Band 10 - With Trumpet
Band 23 - Without Trumpet

FRANCESCO DURANTE
Edited by Bernard Fitzgerald

MUSIC MINUS ONE 50 Executive Boulevard • Elmsford New York 10523-1325